DOMINIC IOCCO

Instill Core Values

Turn core values from a poster into the lifeblood of your organization.

First edition

This book was professionally typeset on Reedsy.
Find out more at reedsy.com

Contents

1

Introduction

I have led or helped lead organizations in a wide variety of arenas, from manufacturing companies to marketing agencies, non-profits, and for-profits. Through all those experiences I have come to believe that the greatest predictor of a healthy organization is whether they have a set of shared core values, that accurately describe how the organization behaves, and are used on a regular basis to build culture.

In fact, if we boil down all the literature over the last decade or so on healthy organizations most of it could be boiled down into one key trait: Do we have a strong set of core values that we live every day?

In my own experience I have found many tools that do a great job of helping any organization quickly develop and define core values. I've consulted with many organizations and can honestly say I can help any group develop a solid set of core values in about 4 hours of focused work. Developing core values is the easy part.

What I have found painfully lacking is practical advice on how to instill core values into an organization so that they truly describe how you behave every day. Creating core values is an exercise in futility if they aren't going to become a key guiding light in how the organization operates.

NOTE: If you've never done this initial step, you can download a simple guide at www.diocco.com.

This book focuses exactly on that, how to effectively take core values and make them the lifeblood of your organization. I'm not going to spend time arguing about the benefits of core values, how to recognize great core values, or how many core values you should have. All of that has been done. But too often some great core values are developed, some posters might be made, and a few attempts to instill them in the culture happen, and then … and then nothing. They sit on nice posters vaguely being referenced, but never being brought to life. I've lived this experience on more than one occasion.

Thus, this book focuses entirely on the nuts and bolts of how to successfully do this, if you are like me, you don't have time to waste, you don't need to be convinced with all the research, you just need practical tools to help fully implement core values in your organization. I will share the lessons I've learned about what works and what doesn't.

In the chapters that follow, we will explore a comprehensive approach to building and nurturing a values-driven culture. We will focus on the most challenging aspect of integrating core values into the fabric of your organization, their daily reinforcement and celebration. We will navigate the pathways that lead to a workplace where values aren't just words on paper but a way of life.

We will discuss how to:

1. Understand the significance of assessing and refining core values to ensure they are a true reflection of your organization's identity and aspirations to ensure a successful launch.
2. Discover the transformative power of living by example and evaluating your leadership team's alignment with these values.
3. Learn to communicate your core values in a way that resonates with employees, making them an integral part of your organizational culture.
4. Understand the psychological dynamics between intrinsic and extrinsic rewards and how to motivate behavior through intrinsic motivation.
5. Explore innovative strategies such as the "$10 Coffee Card Email" and "Company Swag" to celebrate and reinforce core values in action and avoid the pitfalls that commonly affect these approaches.
6. Recognize the importance of personal recognition in expressing gratitude and appreciation for value-driven behavior.
7. Create a culture of transparency and shared commitment where employees share testimonies of value demonstrations.
8. Establish a structured process to ensure alignment with

core values and continuously improve in practice.

9. Develop a method that encourages employees to publicly recognize and celebrate their peers for living core values.

10. Align your hiring, firing, and reward processes with your organization's core values to ensure a consistent and values-driven workforce.

Through real-world examples of lessons learned the hard way, practical insights, and research-backed strategies, this book aims to equip leaders, HR professionals, and employees at all levels with the tools and knowledge needed to cultivate a culture where core values are not just a statement but a way of life.

Join me on this journey towards building a values-driven culture that fosters engagement, inspires innovation, and leaves a lasting impact on your organization, your people, and the world.

2

Review and Refine - The Foundation of Core Values

I n the journey to establish a thriving company culture rooted in core values, the initial step is perhaps the most critical: Creating Core Values. As I mentioned in the introduction there are numerous tools and approaches readily available to walk you through the initial creation of a set of core values.

What I've found more often however is that companies have gone through the exercise of creating core values, but they are sitting somewhere dusty on the shelves and on a never visited link on your website. That's because they've never fully been brought to life in an organization.

In this book I start off assuming you have a set of core values, that you probably haven't read in a while, or that you will go and use one of the tools to create a strong set of values for your organization.

The first step then is to go dig up your core values and read them. Then we need to assess how well they still reflect the organization in front of us today. This process of revisiting and clarifying your organization's core values before embarking on the mission to infuse them into your company's DNA, is critical to avoid a failure to launch exercise that wastes everyone's time and energy.

Understanding the Importance of Core Values

Core values are the guiding principles that define an organization's culture, shape its identity, and influence the behavior of its members. Put simply, core values describe how an organization behaves, both as individuals and as a collective whole. They serve as the compass that points everyone in the right direction, helping to make decisions aligned with the organization's vision and mission.

Many organizations have gone through the exercise of creating core values. Most of the time the values developed are actually a pretty good set of behaviors. Which is why we are skipping the creation of core values in this book. (Again, if you don't have well developed core values there are a ton of resources available, including a simple tool at www.diocco.com).

But if you are like most organizations I've worked with, your core values are a little dusty. Which makes reviewing and refining your core values a crucial step for several reasons. Firstly, as your company evolves, your values may need to evolve too. What was once relevant may not hold the same weight today. Secondly, ensuring that your leadership team is on the same page regarding your core values is paramount. Misalignment among leaders can lead to confusion and inconsistency in how these values are lived within the organization. Third, it's an opportunity to get preliminary buy in from your entire organization.

Involving the Leadership Team

The review process should start with your leadership team, as they play a pivotal role in setting the example for the rest of the organization. Gather your leaders and engage in open, honest, and constructive discussions about your existing core values.

1. Are they still reflective of your company's purpose and beliefs?
2. Are they clear and actionable? Can you describe examples of them in action? Can you describe counter examples that have led to frustration?
3. If we all lived these would this be a great place to work for those who share the values?
4. Do they make your organization truly unique?
5. Does your leadership team behave according to these core values most of the time?

If the answer to any of these is no, then you need to go back and recreate your core values from scratch. If the answer to these questions is mostly yes, then proceed.

Testing Your Core Values

After these discussions, it's time to put your core values to the test. The most critical assessment is to verify that these core values truly reflect how your leadership team mostly behaves day in and day out. Challenge your leadership team to intentionally focus on exemplifying these values for a period, typically two weeks. This exercise not only provides valuable insights into how well these values resonate but also sets a powerful example for others to follow.

However, you can't just tell each other to put them to the test. To really test them, develop a simple sheet that lists the core values on one side and has a column for each day of your test. Each day every member of the leadership team must rate themselves on a scale of 1-5 how well they lived each value that day. Any rating of a 1 or a 5 requires an explanation.

EXAMPLE You can download examples of this sheet, and all the examples mentioned in this book at: www.diocco.com

At the end of the two weeks hold a meeting with the only agenda item being to review the results of this evaluation. Go around the room and have everyone share three things:

1. Overall, did you feel that the core values accurately represent how we want our organization to behave?
2. On a scale of 1 to 5 how well did you live these values? Explain any 1s or 5s, and comment on what the most challenging value to live was.
3. Are you committed to building a culture around these values or do you think we need to go back to the drawing board?

During this review the leader of the organization should be assessing how well he or she believes the team did conducting an honest assessment of the values. The leader should have spent a good part of these two weeks observing the leadership team to see if they truly embody the core values.

The other component the leader needs to be assessing is whether there is full commitment to move forward. The conversation should indicate that the leadership team felt some challenge in living up to the core values, but that most of the time they did behave accordingly. What would be a red flag is everyone just agreeing to move forward, if this exercise didn't spark some initial enthusiasm for seeing the whole organization behaving this way, then go back to the drawing board.

Aligning for Success

Once your leadership team has reviewed and tested the core values, it's essential to ensure everyone is aligned. Make any necessary refinements to the language and content of your values to reflect the collective understanding and commitment. Most organizations I've worked with find it necessary to create 3-5 bullet points for each core value to clearly articulate what exactly living that value at work looks like. When everyone is on the same page, it becomes easier to communicate and implement these values throughout the organization.

Optional but Highly Recommended – The whole organization review

Once you have what you believe are nearly finished core values, a valuable step can be to bring them to the entire organization, ideally in a large group meeting. During this meeting the leader should explain the honest history of core values in the organization, why core values are critical to the future success of the organization, and how you are about to review them for refinement.

WARNING: If you aren't 100% honest about the history of core values in the organization, or if you can't explain in a compelling manner why they are critical moving forward, everyone will tune you out and this exercise will be futile.

Now, pass out the current draft of core values, it should clearly read DRAFT on the page, and go through them one at a time. Ask some of the following questions for each value, and each bullet point of the value:

1. Is it clear?
2. Can someone give me a recent example of this in action?
3. Are there better ways to articulate what we are trying to get at with this statement?

As the questions are being answered, notes must be taken with an eye towards including some of the thoughts and suggestions in the final iteration of your core values.

WARNING: If you do this step, you must make some tweaks to your core values that employees will recognize so that they know they had a hand in shaping them. Your team will invariably have some great ideas that will help refine what you thought was perfectly clear in a way that makes more sense to everyone. If you aren't willing to do that skip this step entirely.

This process will create significantly more buy-in to the work you will now begin of instilling the core values in your organization. It ensures that your values remain relevant, actionable, and aligned with your organizational goals. With a well-defined and thoroughly reviewed set of core values, you are now ready to take the next step: Living Witness.

3

Living Witness - Lead by Example

The next step of our journey towards building a robust company culture driven by core values is dedicated to "Living Witness." This pivotal step emphasizes the importance of setting a strong example, starting within your leadership team, and evaluating each member's commitment to the core values before officially announcing them to the wider organization.

"Modern man listens more willingly to witnesses than to teachers, and if he does listen to teachers, it is because they are witnesses," - Pope Paul VI, 1975

As Pope Paul VI articulated 50 years ago, your witness matters far more than anything you say. Being a living witness is about embodying the core values in every aspect of your leadership team's actions and decisions, and honestly assessing where and when we fall short. This sets the tone for the entire organization, creating a culture deeply rooted in these essential principles. If a leader consistently fails to live up to one or more of your core values, the whole effort is doomed to fail. There are only two solutions to that problem:

1. That person is a bad fit and needs to go.
2. Your core values aren't accurate and need to be refined.

The Two-Week Immersion Period

This is essentially the same exercise described in the last chapter. If you faithfully executed that step, and your core values didn't significantly change after you reviewed them with the whole organization, then you can safely skip this step.

If that's not the case, then before announcing your core values to the entire company, dedicate two weeks to immerse your leadership team in a culture that lives and breathes these values. During this period, leaders should consciously apply and evaluate themselves, and each other on how these values were lived in their daily work and interactions. This immersion serves multiple purposes: it allows leaders to experience firsthand how these values can guide decisions, and it also acts as a form of internal alignment.

Follow the same format as outlined in the first chapter with one additional component. At the end of this two-week period, it's time for everyone on the leadership team to honestly evaluate themselves and every other member of the leadership team. Have they demonstrated a commitment to the core values during this immersion? Are they leading by example? This evaluation should be objective, fair, and constructive, focusing on behaviors rather than personal attributes.

Leadership team members who exemplify the core values serve as role models for the entire organization. They provide tangible proof that these values are not just words on paper but actionable principles that guide decision-making and behavior. This sets a powerful precedent for employees at all levels.

Living Witness also instills a sense of accountability within the leadership team. When they actively participate in living the core values, they become more invested in the successful implementation of these values throughout the organization. This accountability extends beyond the leadership team and spreads to all employees as the culture takes shape.

After this initial period, it's critical that the leadership team reevaluates their behavior on a regular basis, at a minimum annually. Being a Living Witness is not just a theoretical exercise but a transformative journey. It sets the stage for a culture where core values are not just discussed but lived and breathed by everyone. With the leadership team serving as living witnesses to the values, you're now well-prepared to move on to the next chapter: Communicate.

4

Over Communicate

E ffective communication of these values is paramount to ensure that they become a part of your organization's DNA, guiding behaviors and shaping the way your company operates. If you are reading this book, I will assume you know that sending an email with your new core values is not an option. I assume you also know the adage that people must hear something at least 7 times before they hear it for the first time. To make core values an integral part of your culture I'd argue that number is closer to 70 times.

The Power of Clear Communication

Core values serve as the foundation of your company culture, defining how everyone should behave and make decisions. However, these values can only influence your organization if they are effectively communicated and understood by all.

Start by communicating your core values transparently and with utmost clarity. Employees need to understand what each value means in practical terms and how they should manifest in their day-to-day work. Use clear and simple language to describe each value and provide examples to illustrate how they translate into action.

A critical step in the communication process is making a company-wide announcement. Gather your entire organization and explain that these core values represent the compass by which your company navigates its journey. Emphasize that these values are not just ideals but the way everyone should behave at work.

This meeting should be 45 minutes to an hour long and requires that the leader prepare a strong speech going through each core value slowly and in detail. But to make it truly effective, each core value needs an example of an employee living this value in action. This isn't a hypothetical example, it's a concrete example that happened. This step accomplishes two great things. First, it makes the core value clear and tangible. Second, it provides a moment of special recognition for the employees that reminds them how much the leader notices and cares for them as individuals, there is no better way to start the implementation of values in an organization with a positive experience and public recognition.

WARNING: Avoid the temptation to feel like you must include every employee as an example. Hopefully, your organization is too large to make this even possible. But in small to midsize organizations this is a real temptation. But I can assure you that if you are like most organizations there are a few people on the team who do not live out the core values in any meaningful way, more on them later. By highlighting someone everyone knows, and believe me they know better than you, doesn't live up to these values you will have sabotaged the importance of truly living them before you've even really started.

To make core values tangible and relatable, provide specific examples of how they apply in various situations. Share stories of employees who have exemplified these values and the positive impact it had on the organization. Use real-life scenarios to illustrate how employees can live these values in their roles.

Communicating core values effectively is the start of embedding them into your company culture, but it's only a start. One great speech won't make them come alive. It's not just about articulating these values but ensuring that they become ingrained in how your organization operates. With clear, repeated, communication, real-life examples, and consistent reinforcement, you pave the way for these values to guide your organization towards success. As you continue your journey, remember that the communication of core values is an ongoing effort that requires commitment and dedication from all members of your organization.

5

Intrinsic vs. Extrinsic Rewards

Before we delve into specific action items to ingrain the core values into your culture a warning is in order. We need to discuss the dynamics between intrinsic and extrinsic rewards within the context of core values. Understanding the research-backed principles behind how people respond to these rewards is essential in fostering a culture where individuals are motivated by a deeper sense of purpose and alignment with organizational values, rather than relying on financial incentives. While you should financially reward employees over the long-term that exemplify your core values, in the short term, and as a method of ingraining the core values into a culture you should lean heavily on intrinsic rewards.

The Science of Motivation

Research in the fields of psychology and organizational behavior has shed light on the factors that motivate individuals in the workplace. One of the fundamental distinctions made by researchers is between intrinsic and extrinsic motivation.

Intrinsic motivation refers to the internal desire to engage in an activity or behavior because it is inherently enjoyable, interesting, or aligned with one's personal values. On the other hand, extrinsic motivation involves external rewards, such as bonuses, promotions, which drive individuals to perform tasks.

Studies have consistently shown that intrinsic rewards, such as personal satisfaction, a sense of accomplishment, and alignment with one's values, are potent drivers of long-term engagement and commitment. When individuals feel that their work is meaningful and aligned with their core values, they are more likely to be motivated and dedicated to their tasks.

Contrastingly, excessive reliance on extrinsic rewards, such as financial bonuses, can have unintended consequences. Extrinsic rewards often diminish intrinsic motivation, as they may be perceived as controlling or manipulative. Employees may begin to focus solely on the rewards, rather than the value of their work or the alignment with core values.

The key to creating a culture that values intrinsic motivation is to strike a balance between intrinsic and extrinsic rewards. While extrinsic rewards can play a role in recognizing and appreciating employees' efforts over the long-term, they should not overshadow the significance of intrinsic rewards derived from living core values. The real challenge lies in fostering an environment where employees are intrinsically motivated by their alignment with the organization's values.

By emphasizing the intrinsic rewards derived from alignment with values, organizations can create a more engaged, committed, and values-driven workforce, contributing to long-term success and sustainability. The research on motivation underscores the importance of nurturing intrinsic motivation as a cornerstone of a thriving organizational culture.

6

The Gift Card and Email Tactic

Oone of the classic examples you'll find for reinforcing core values within your organization is the weekly gift card and email program. This innovative approach combines recognition, reward, and communication to celebrate and encourage the consistent demonstration of your core values.

Recognition is a fundamental human need, and it plays a pivotal role in reinforcing desired behaviors within an organization. Multiple studies have found that companies with effective recognition programs have much lower voluntary turnover rates. Recognizing employees for embodying core values not only boosts morale but also encourages others to follow suit.

The Gift Card/Email Concept

The concept is simple yet powerful. The first week someone from the leadership team identifies an employee who does something that exemplifies the core value. This leader then proceeds to send a company wide email explaining what happened and that the employee is receiving a gift card for the behavior. They also explain that this employee now has the ball in their court, over the next week they will be watching for behavior in another employee that exemplifies a core value, send a company wide email, and that person gets a gift card. Ideally, this process repeats every week.

This recognition system serves multiple purposes. It publicly acknowledges individuals who embody the core values, reinforcing the importance of those values within the organization. Furthermore, it highlights specific examples of the values in action, making them more tangible and relatable to all employees.

The size of the gift card is also kept intentionally low, generally $10-25, to make it less likely to become a purely financial incentive. With the repeating cycle of the person who received the gift card paying it forward creates a positive feedback loop that continuously reinforces the values throughout the organization.

It all sounds great in theory, but I've rarely seen it remain effective past the first month or two. The most common problem is that it can quickly descend into a game of favorites, I like this person, so I'm going to give them the card. Additionally, depending on the organization, the email and its focus on articulating and representing one of the core values can quickly diminish.

To make this approach truly effective I suggest the following tweaks based on my experience:

1. Make it a $10 Coffee Gift card (there's no need for the amount to be any higher), or better yet see the company swag chapter and combine it with a value thermos.
2. Coordinate the entire effort through someone in leadership. This could be a manager, HR, etc. Before the weekly email is sent and a gift awarded have the employee meet with this person in order to ensure the following: that the action truly embodied a core value, and that the email clearly communicates and reiterates the core value, in fact I'd have the same leadership team member that starts the process, send the email every week in order to ensure the program continues and consistent reinforcement is maintained.

The Gift Card/Email idea is a practical and effective tool for celebrating core values in action. It harnesses the power of recognition to motivate employees to live by these values consistently. By making the values visible, tangible, and rewarding, you create a culture where everyone is invested in upholding the core principles that define your organization. But it requires some tweaks to the standard protocol to make it an effective and lasting program.

7

Company Swag - Wearing Core Values with Pride

Who doesn't love company swag? T-shirts, hats, mugs can all be used as a creative and engaging way to reinforce your organization's core values. By creating custom company t-shirts that prominently feature these values, you can not only raise awareness but also cultivate a sense of pride and identity among your employees. Take a page from college basketball programs with their warmups boldly proclaiming a central theme.

The Power of Visual Representation

Core values are intangible concepts that guide behavior and decision-making. However, making them tangible through visual representation can have a profound impact. A lot of companies make beautiful posters, in one company we even made some cool banners that hung in the factory, the problem with these visual approaches is that they quickly become part of the furniture, and then no one notices them.

I think a better approach is to create attractive company swag that features your core values, by doing this you're giving employees a constant reminder of the principles they should embody, that don't become just part of the everyday furniture.

The design of your company swag is crucial. It should be eye-catching, easily recognizable, and clearly feature your core values. Incorporate colors, logos, or symbols that are associated with your values to create a strong visual connection. This can include creating company t-shirts, hats (though these require real creativity to get right), or other wearable or everyday carry items that employees can proudly display. Done right, this not only promotes the core values, but serves as a great marketing piece when employees use the items in public.

Company t-shirts featuring core values become conversation starters. When employees wear them in and outside the workplace, it prompts discussions about what these values mean and how they apply to daily work and interactions.

Distributing the company swag can be an event. Host a launch event or a team-building activity where employees receive their shirts. Or better yet, don't give out the swag to everyone, use it as another tool to honor someone who did something specific to live out the core value. This not only builds anticipation but also fosters a sense of community as everyone proudly dons their new award.

When employees wear their company swag, it creates a sense of belonging and unity. They identify themselves as part of a team that shares common values and beliefs. This unity can strengthen teamwork, collaboration, and alignment with the organization's mission.

Encourage employees to wear their company swag during special occasions or team-building events. This serves as a visual reminder of the values that underpin your organization and provides an opportunity to celebrate and recognize individuals who consistently live by these values.

Custom company t-shirts give employees a sense of ownership in the company culture. They take pride in representing their organization and its values, both within the workplace and in their personal lives.

To ensure the longevity of this approach, periodically refresh the design of the company swag to keep it appealing and relevant. Create a new shirt each year, maybe designed by an employee, which can turn them into nearly a collector's item. Additionally, consider creating new swag items beyond t-shirts, such as mugs, bags, or hats, to provide variety and keep the excitement alive.

Company swag featuring your core values is a creative and impactful way to reinforce these principles within your organization and market it beyond your organization. By designing and distributing items that employees are proud to wear, you create a tangible connection between your workforce and the values that define your company.

8

Personal Email - The Power of Individual Recognition

I n this chapter, we finally find a good use for email, it can be used as an effective means of recognizing and reinforcing core values within your organization. Simple yet heartfelt, personal emails can have a profound impact on employees by acknowledging their commitment to the organization's values.

Recognition is a cornerstone of a thriving organizational culture. Research reveals that employees who feel appreciated are more engaged, motivated, and committed to their work. Personal email is a direct, personal, timely, and easy way to express gratitude and acknowledge individuals who exemplify core values.

A personal email goes beyond a generic "thank you" message. It allows leaders and colleagues to connect with employees on an individual level. It demonstrates that their efforts are not only noticed but also valued by the organization.

When recognizing someone for living core values, tailor the email to include specific details about their actions and contributions. Highlight the impact their behavior had on the team or the organization. Be genuine and specific in your praise. You can do all of this in 3-4 sentences.

Personal emails provide immediate acknowledgment. When you witness an employee embodying a core value, send the email promptly, within the hour if possible but absolutely within 24 hours. Timely recognition reinforces the behavior and encourages its repetition.

The act of receiving a personal email for demonstrating core values reinforces the desired behavior. It sends a clear message that the organization values and prioritizes these principles, encouraging individuals to continue living by them.

Personal emails can also initiate a dialogue. They provide an opportunity for recipients to share their thoughts, ideas, or concerns, fostering open communication and strengthening the organizational culture.

One of the strengths of personal email recognition is its immediacy. When a colleague or supervisor witnesses a fellow employee exemplifying a core value, they can promptly send a personal email to acknowledge and thank them for their contribution. This quick response reinforces the behavior and motivates the employee to continue living the values.

In a world inundated with digital communication, the power of a personal email should not be underestimated. It is a simple yet effective way to recognize and appreciate employees for embodying your organization's core values. As you continue your journey to instill these values in your company culture, remember that personal emails create a lasting impression and promote a culture of recognition and gratitude.

9

Handwritten Note - Elevating Recognition with a Personal Touch

Taking the concept of a personal email to the next level involves sending handwritten notes as a powerful way to recognize and appreciate employees for demonstrating your organization's core values. The personal touch of a handwritten note adds depth and authenticity to your recognition efforts, fostering a stronger emotional connection between leadership and employees.

Handwritten notes have a unique charm that digital messages cannot replicate. The effort and care invested in crafting a handwritten message sends a powerful message of genuine appreciation. In a fast-paced, digital world, receiving a handwritten note is a memorable and cherished experience.

One of the primary strengths of handwritten notes is their personalization. You can tailor each note to the individual and the specific core value they exemplified. This level of thoughtfulness demonstrates a deep understanding of the employee's contributions and reinforces the value in question.

A handwritten note is unexpected and delightful, making it even more impactful. Employees often do not anticipate such gestures, and when they receive one, it serves as a pleasant surprise that brightens their day and boosts morale.

A handwritten note is tangible recognition—an artifact that employees can keep and revisit. It serves as a lasting reminder of their accomplishments and the appreciation they received for living the core values. Many employees proudly display such notes at their workstations as a source of motivation, which in turn is noticed by other employees.

Handwritten notes provide an opportunity to express gratitude sincerely. You can convey your appreciation in your own words, sharing how the employee's actions aligned with the organization's core values and made a positive impact.

Sending handwritten notes fosters a deeper connection between leadership and employees. It shows that leaders take the time to acknowledge and celebrate individual contributions, which, in turn, strengthens the bond between team members.

Consistent recognition through handwritten notes reinforces the importance of core values within the organization. When employees receive handwritten notes for living these values, it encourages them to continue doing so and sets a standard for behavior across the organization.

If you really want to take this practice to the next level,

have custom postcards designed that communicate your core values. Use these cards to send the note, and only for this purpose. While this step isn't necessary, overtime it will become immediately recognizable.

10

Staff Meeting Opening - Celebrating Core Values Together

One of the cheapest, easiest, and most effective ways to reinforce core values is to start all meetings with the prompt, "Who has a shout out for someone living out our core values?" This five-minute exercise is a great way to reinforce these principles and create a sense of shared purpose and commitment among team members.

The way you start a meeting often sets the tone for the entire gathering. By beginning staff meetings with a focus on core values, you send a clear message that these principles are central to your organization's culture and daily operations.

A powerful way to integrate core values into staff meetings is by sharing testimonies of individuals who have recently demonstrated these values. These stories serve as real-life examples of how the values are put into action and highlight the positive impact they have on the organization.

Testimonies not only celebrate the values but also inspire and motivate employees. Hearing about their colleagues' successes in living the core values can instill a sense of pride, motivation, and a desire to emulate these behaviors.

Opening meetings with core value testimonies creates a safe space for employees to share their experiences and recognize their peers. It encourages a culture of open communication and reinforces the idea that everyone plays a role in upholding the organization's values.

Incorporating peer recognition into staff meetings fosters a sense of belonging and camaraderie. When employees witness their colleagues being acknowledged for their commitment to core values, it reinforces the importance of these principles and encourages others to follow suit.

Leadership should actively participate in the process by sharing their own stories of how they've seen someone live out the core values. This not only sets an example but also demonstrates that everyone, regardless of their position, is accountable for living these values.

By highlighting core values at the beginning of meetings, you ensure that these principles are continuously aligned with your organization's goals and objectives. It reinforces the idea that success is not only measured by financial outcomes but also by how well the values are lived.

Consistently incorporating core values into staff meetings contributes to building a values-driven culture. It reinforces the idea that these principles are not just slogans but are integral to decision-making and behavior within the organization.

Starting staff meetings with a focus on core values is a powerful and arguably the simplest way to reinforce these principles and create a shared sense of purpose among team members. Begin meetings with a spotlight on core values, providing a platform for recognition, inspiration, and alignment with your organization's mission and goals.

11

Department Review - Self-Assessment for Living Core Values

H aving, communicating, recognizing, and acknowledging core values in action is a great start, but we also need to find ways to continuously improve. The "Department Review" is a structured approach to evaluating how different departments within your organization are aligning with and living your core values. This self-assessment process promotes accountability, transparency, and continuous improvement in integrating values into departmental operations.

To ensure that your organization's core values are consistently practiced, it's essential to evaluate how each department is incorporating these principles into their day-to-day work. Departmental alignment is crucial for maintaining a cohesive and values-driven culture throughout the entire organization.

Develop a comprehensive review sheet that outlines key aspects of living the core values within each department. This sheet should include specific criteria and indicators that reflect how well the values are integrated into departmental processes, decision-making, and interactions.

Make department heads accountable for their respective departments' alignment with core values. Require them to conduct regular self-assessments using the review sheet and encourage them to involve their team members in the process. This collaborative approach ensures that employees at all levels are engaged in evaluating and improving their department's adherence to values.

The key to making this process work however is that you must require department heads to report their self-assessment results to the leadership team on a regular basis. Without this step too many people will skip over or rush through the process to deal with the more pressing matters. This reporting mechanism fosters transparency and allows leadership to gain insights into how values are being lived across the organization, but more than anything it ensures that it is regularly happening. It also provides opportunities for leadership to offer guidance and support to departments that may be facing challenges in alignment.

Acknowledge and celebrate departments that consistently demonstrate a strong commitment to core values. Highlight their achievements in living these values as examples for other departments to follow. Recognition serves as motivation and reinforces the importance of values-driven behavior.

The departmental review process should not only focus on

successes but should identify areas where improvement is needed. Use the insights gained from self-assessments to create action plans for departments to enhance their alignment with core values. Encourage collaboration between departments to share best practices and strategies.

In one organization I worked with each department would conduct this review and then select one core value to work on for the next month. Before leaving the meeting, they would discuss ideas on how they individually and as a department could really focus on living out that particular value better.

Hold department heads accountable for implementing the action plans and tracking progress toward better alignment with core values. Regularly revisit the self-assessment process to evaluate improvements and make necessary adjustments.

Recognize that the alignment of departments with core values is an ongoing process. As your organization evolves, so too should the criteria and indicators used for assessment. Continuously seek feedback from employees and department heads to adapt and refine the review process.

Implementing a structured Department Review process for evaluating alignment with core values is a crucial step in creating a values-driven organization that is constantly improving. By engaging department heads and employees in assessing their own adherence to these principles, you foster accountability, transparency, and a commitment to continuous improvement.

12

The Shout Out Wall - Celebrating Core Values Publicly

Another effective means of reinforcing your core values is the "Shout Out Wall," an engaging and interactive way to celebrate and recognize individuals and teams for their consistent demonstration of your organization's core values. This visual display fosters a sense of pride, encourages positive behavior, and promotes a values-driven culture.

Public recognition holds a special place in fostering a positive organizational culture. When employees witness their colleagues being acknowledged for living core values, it not only celebrates individual achievements but also reinforces the importance of these values within the organization.

Designate a physical space within your workplace, this could be as simple as a bulletin board or as elaborate dedicated digital kiosk, as the "Shout Out Wall." This is where employees can post shout-outs celebrating the core value demonstration of their colleagues.

Encourage employees to submit shout-outs when they witness a colleague exemplifying a core value in action. Provide a simple template or digital form for shout-out submissions, allowing individuals to describe the observed behavior and its impact on the organization.

Make the Shout Out Wall accessible to everyone in the organization. Ensure that it is a space where employees from all departments and levels can participate, fostering the greatest visibility.

Keep the Shout Out Wall up to date by regularly posting new shout-outs. This can only be done if the submission process is kept very simple. If it's a bulletin board, have a stack of custom postcards and pens available ready to post, if it's digital make sure everyone has quick and easy access to the form. This ensures that the recognition remains fresh and ongoing, and that everyone can be celebrated for their commitment to core values. This also helps prevent it from becoming part of the furniture as mentioned before.

The visual impact of the Shout Out Wall cannot be underestimated. When employees see their peers' shout-outs displayed prominently, it reinforces the values as a collective effort and encourages others to engage in similar behavior.

The Shout Out Wall can also introduce a healthy sense of competition in a positive way. Employees may be inspired to earn shout-outs and contribute to the culture of recognition within the organization. In addition to individual shout-outs, the Shout Out Wall can be used to celebrate teams or departments that consistently live by the core values.

Leadership should actively participate in the Shout Out Wall initiative by contributing shout outs and leading by example. The leadership team should establish a goal of individually posting 2-3 shout outs per month. When leaders publicly recognize employees for their value-based actions, it reinforces the importance of these principles throughout the organization.

Consider hosting recognition events where shout outs from the Shout Out Wall are celebrated in a more formal setting. This provides an opportunity to publicly acknowledge employees and showcase their contributions.

The Shout Out Wall is a dynamic and interactive way to celebrate and recognize employees who consistently demonstrate your organization's core values. And the shout outs posted can be repurposed into some of the other tactics, like the opening of meetings.

13

Hire, Fire, Reward - Cultivating Core Values through Talent Management

U ltimately, core values will only permeate your organization when they drive all hiring, firing, and rewarding decisions in a values-driven organization. Aligning these processes with your core values is critical to the long-term success of their implementation.

Hiring, firing, and rewarding employees are fundamental aspects of talent management that directly impact your organization's culture. Ensuring that these processes align with your core values is essential for maintaining a values-driven workplace.

The most complicated area to implement this is during the hiring process. Trying to identify candidates who share your organization's core values can seem daunting but is crucial to saving headaches down the road. To achieve this, you can incorporate specific interview questions that assess a candidate's alignment with these principles. Here are some simple examples of interview questions designed to get at a core value fit:

1. Teamwork: "Can you share an experience where you went above and beyond to support a colleague or contribute to a team project? What motivated you to take that extra step?"

2. Integrity (By the way this is a terrible core value, if someone doesn't have integrity, they shouldn't be working for you): "Describe a situation where you faced a moral or ethical dilemma at work. How did you handle it, and what values guided your decision-making process?"

3. Innovation: "Tell us about a time when you came up with an innovative solution to a problem at home. How did you come up with it and did it work?"

4. Customer Focus: "Share an experience where you went out of your way to ensure a positive customer experience. How does delivering exceptional service align with your personal values?"

5. Accountability: "Describe a project where you took ownership of a mistake or challenge. How did you hold yourself accountable, and how did your boss react?"

By asking questions that delve into candidates' values and their alignment with your organization's core values, you increase the likelihood of bringing in individuals who will contribute positively to your culture.

Firing and Values Misalignment

Sometimes, despite efforts to hire individuals who align with your core values, values misalignment may still occur. In such cases, it's essential to address the issue promptly. Be transparent about how the employee's actions or behavior contradict the organization's values and provide a brief opportunity for improvement (30-90 days).

There is plenty written on the importance of firing quickly, so I won't elaborate this point much more. But once you have a set of solid core values, I am willing to bet nearly all your personnel challenges will boil down to bad alignment of core values. Move on quickly.

Rewarding for Values Demonstration

We've spent most of this book looking at specific ways to reward employees in the short-term for demonstrating core values. In the long term your annual reviews, raises, and promotions should all be tied to employees who consistently demonstrate your core values.

Hire, fire, and reward processes are critical elements of talent management that can significantly influence your organization's culture and values. By aligning these processes with your core values and using thoughtful interview questions to assess candidates' alignment during the hiring process, you can build and maintain a values-driven workplace.

14

Sustaining a Values-Driven Culture

As we conclude this journey through the intricacies of building and nurturing a values-driven culture, we arrive at a destination where core values are not just words on a wall, but the heart and soul of an organization. If you apply 2 or 3 of these ideas across your organization consistently core values will become the driving behavior of your organization. You do not need to implement them all, and you can easily connect several of them to help reinforce their effect. What you must do is commit to consistently using 2-3 of them.

The impact of a values-driven culture extends far beyond the workplace. It resonates with customers, partners, and the broader community, fostering trust and loyalty. It contributes to social responsibility and sustainability, as organizations guided by values prioritize not only profits but also the well-being of society and the environment.

Leaders play a pivotal role in sustaining a values-driven culture.

They must lead by example, consistently embodying the core values in their actions and decisions. Effective communication and transparency are essential, ensuring that values are integrated into the organization's DNA and not just a poster on the wall.

Accountability is the cornerstone of a values-driven culture. It involves holding all employees, from top to bottom, responsible for living and upholding the core values. Creating mechanisms for regular self-assessment, peer evaluation, and departmental reviews ensures that values remain at the forefront of decision-making.

In closing, I acknowledge that building and sustaining a values-driven culture is a dynamic and ongoing endeavor. It is also never the most pressing item on a leader's plate. It is not without its challenges, but the rewards are immeasurable. A values-driven culture fosters engagement, inspires innovation, attracts top talent, and ultimately drives long-term success.

I hope this book has provided you with valuable insights, strategies, and inspiration to embark on or continue your journey towards a values-driven culture. Remember that core values are the guiding stars that illuminate your path, and by staying true to them, you can create a workplace that not only excels in business but also leaves a positive and lasting impact on the world.